Think Happy, Be Happy

A Book of Joyous Living

KIRSTIE SHAPIRO

Copyright © 2022 Kirstie Shapiro.

All rights reserved. No part of this book may be used or reproduced by any means, graphic, electronic, or mechanical, including photocopying, recording, taping or by any information storage retrieval system without the written permission of the author except in the case of brief quotations embodied in critical articles and reviews.

Balboa Press books may be ordered through booksellers or by contacting:

Balboa Press
A Division of Hay House
1663 Liberty Drive
Bloomington, IN 47403
www.balboapress.com
844-682-1282

Because of the dynamic nature of the Internet, any web addresses or links contained in this book may have changed since publication and may no longer be valid. The views expressed in this work are solely those of the author and do not necessarily reflect the views of the publisher, and the publisher hereby disclaims any responsibility for them.

The author of this book does not dispense medical advice or prescribe the use of any technique as a form of treatment for physical, emotional, or medical problems without the advice of a physician, either directly or indirectly. The intent of the author is only to offer information of a general nature to help you in your quest for emotional and spiritual well-being. In the event you use any of the information in this book for yourself, which is your constitutional right, the author and the publisher assume no responsibility for your actions.

Any people depicted in stock imagery provided by Getty Images are models, and such images are being used for illustrative purposes only. Certain stock imagery © Getty Images.

Print information available on the last page.

ISBN: 979-8-7652-2720-6 (sc)
ISBN: 979-8-7652-2718-3 (hc)
ISBN: 979-8-7652-2719-0 (e)

Library of Congress Control Number: 2022906618

Balboa Press rev. date: 11/08/2022

Foreword

I met Kirstie thirteen years ago during one of my *Be Your Potential* seminars.

I meet hundreds of people every year through running events, yet I still remember the day I met Kirstie. She instantly emits a presence and energy of warmth, passion, and love for life.

It's been a delight to watch her grow and develop over the years, becoming a manifestation of her true potential.

I am so thrilled and honoured to be promoting her book, as she is one of those special people who live by what they preach and is so full of love that it seems to ooze from her pores.

Her true passion is to teach love to all she meets. This I love.

I just know that by reading this book and going through the positive statements, you too will find the joy and love in abundance that Kirstie wants all of us to experience every day of our lives.

It's all within you.

Joseph Clough
Bestselling author of *Be Your Potential*

Preface

Happiness and Joy: where do they come from, and how are they created?

The simple answer is that happiness lies within you and the choices you make every moment of every single day.

It all starts with creating a positive and happy inner voice and allowing that inner voice to shine out of you into the world for all to see and be inspired by. This gives permission for everyone to set themselves free.

Happiness, like any other manifestation or state of being, is a regular internal check of your thoughts, inner dialogue, and actions.

With this book, I share with you some of my own personal thoughts, inspirations, and ideas that have helped me create a life of pure joy.

I hope that they will resonate with the light within to help you create, experience, and live a life full of wonder and happiness.

Wishing you Peace and Love with all my heart,
Kirstie Shapiro

This book is dedicated to my beautiful daughter Kiana Lula, who inspires me to be more than I ever dreamed possible.

I Love you, My Darling.

The Light is within You.

Shine.

You are in control of your own Happiness.
It is your choice and no one else's.

Peace & Love

The most joyous way to celebrate Love,
In all its forms,
Is to give it freely and unconditionally.

Peace & Love

Do you realise just how beautiful and amazing you are?
Look in the mirror.
Look deep inside your heart.
Now find ten beautiful things about yourself and say:
Thank you.

Peace & Love

Rejoice in each moment.
There is no other like it!

Peace & Love

Happiness is a Perception.
If you are not Happy,
Change your Perception of your world.
Discover your Happiness.

Peace & Love

Yippee!
Another day to Delight in.

Peace & Love

Nothing exterior to you can bring Happiness.
Happiness is found only within you.
It is you, and you are Love.

Peace & Love

Each experience grows from a seed of thought.
Lovingly guide your thoughts.
Nurture them with Kindness.

Peace & Love

You cannot find Happiness somewhere else
Until you are Happy where you are,
And with who you are.

Peace & Love

Forgiveness of others,
Forgiveness of circumstance,
Forgiveness of Self,
This is the way to create a Peaceful, Loving and Fulfilling life.

Peace & Love

In the great words of the late John Lennon,
Love is the answer.

Peace & Love

Love, and let go.
Love, and let go.
This is the path of Happiness.

Peace & Love

Breathe.
Be present.
Smile upon your thoughts, release them.
Be present.
Slowly and steadily do, say, create.
Be present.

Peace & Love

Anger blinds us from the Beauty that is present.
Laugh with anger and be Healed.

Peace & Love

When you lose someone to death,
To another, or to circumstance,
Give thanks for the good times shared.
In the loss, you learn to Love wholly without regret.

Peace & Love

Have goals, but let life take care of the details.
Enjoy the journey.
Take time to Smile,
Laugh, and
Be.

Peace & Love

Be present,
Totally and completely.
Be present in each moment.
You may not always get this right,
But when you do,
Life is Magical and Divine.

Peace & Love

To really know and understand yourself takes gentle kindness
And compassion towards yourself.

Peace & Love

Learn something new.
Be creative.
Get out of your comfort zone.
Feel more Alive!

Peace & Love

Take time to get to know people.
Embrace others with warmth and love.
Treat them with importance.
This brings great contentedness.

Peace & Love

Action is always worth the effort.
No effort, No action, No progress.

Peace & Love

Every moment is an experience.
Be present.
Embrace each moment,
Just as it is,
And then let it go.

Peace & Love

Expanding, exploring, discovering, and learning.
Breathing, being, loving, and laughing.
These are the Joys of Living life.

Peace & Love

Harsh words cannot be retracted.
Stop! Be present.
Keep a gentle watch of your thoughts.
Take a gentle care of your speech.

Peace & Love

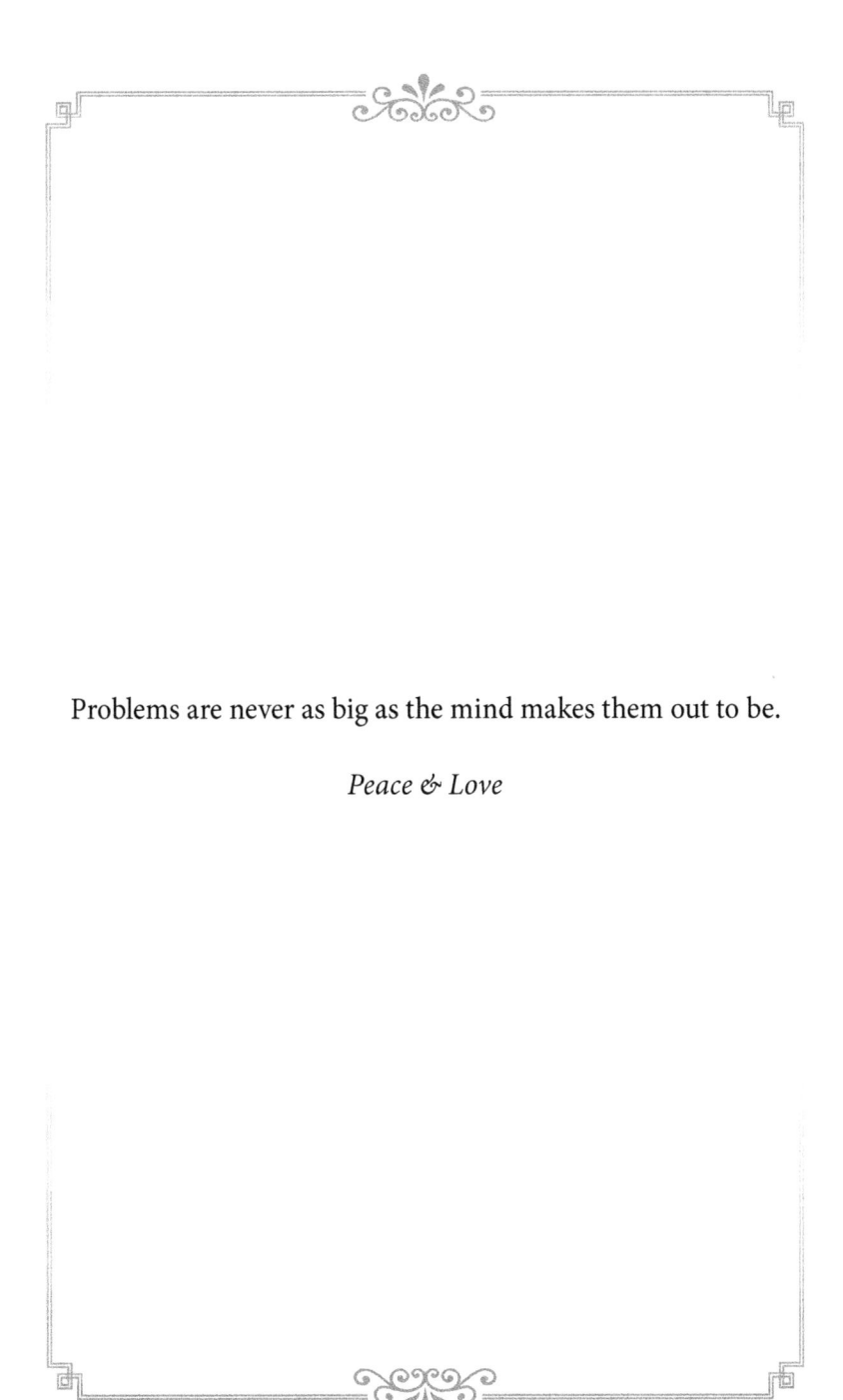

Problems are never as big as the mind makes them out to be.

Peace & Love

It is good to take time out to mend the body.
The mind and heart will get a little time out too.

Peace & Love

Compassion, Tolerance, and Love
Are the recipe for a
Happy, Contented, and Fulfilling life.

Peace & Love

To know right action, look within.
If it is right, your heart will rejoice.
If it is not right, your heart will be at dis-ease.

Peace & Love

Sometimes the purpose in life is simply to be.
Relax and exult in being.

Peace & Love

A little understanding can bring great compassion.
And with this a touch more tolerance.

Peace & Love

Leap into life with complete abandon.
Soak up every moment of Joy!

Peace & Love

With true understanding comes unconditional
Love, Support, and Compassion.
Drink from this cup.
Quench your thirst.

Peace & Love

The joy of new life is such a Blessing!
Our young are so Precious, Pure, and Beautiful,
Our time with them is transient.

Peace & Love

Material possessions mean nothing.
They don't bring Happiness, Enlightenment, or Wisdom.
They can bring comfort and great fun!

Peace & Love

Pain is caused by focusing on the past
And on things we don't have.
Focus instead on this moment and on what you do have.

Peace & Love

Passing on and sharing knowledge is a key to Happiness.

Peace & Love

Treat every person as if they are your best friend.
Treat your friends as if they are the most precious treasures.

Peace & Love

You never know whose life you are impacting,
Act with gentle Kindness, Love, and Compassion
Always.

Peace & Love

Your past is never as bad as it could have been.
Be grateful, move on, be present.
Give thanks for everything.

Peace & Love

The mind has an incredible capacity for distortion.
May the mind always distort memories and events,
Positively and Happily.

Peace & Love

I am slowly discovering life to be
A playground of Potentiality and Bliss.

Peace & Love

Every day, every moment, every person
Is to be savoured and enjoyed.

Peace & Love

You get one chance at this day, this experience, this moment. Make the most of it.

Peace & Love

The universe is abundance.
Open your heart to gratitude,
See it everywhere.

Peace & Love

It is always in the small things we find the greatest treasure:
A Smile, a Laugh, a Look, a Touch, a Kindness.

Peace & Love

Simple tasks can bring great Joy.
Nurture houseplants.
Tend the garden.
Clean the house.
Be present.
Approach all things positively
And with the right mental attitude.
Find peace in these profound experiences.

Peace & Love

The path to Happiness is in Forgiveness.
Forgive readily and easily.

Peace & Love

Love is everything.
Love is everywhere.

Peace & Love

What you eat makes a difference
To how you Feel, Think, and Act.
Choose wisely what you put in your body.

Peace & Love

Breathe,
Smile,
Go gently about your day,
One step at a time,
Gracefully making your way through life.

Peace & Love

Own your responses and reactions to outside stimuli.
It's all a reflection of what lies within.

Peace & Love

Today is the day for
Doing, Saying, and Being
All that you are.

Peace & Love

Gratitude exists in each thing in every moment.
Open your eyes, simply see it.

Peace & Love

You get one go at this life.
Make sure that the people you Love
Know that you Love them.

Peace & Love

Small deeds of Kindness
Often have great value for the receiver.

Peace & Love

Sometimes our hearts experience sadness.
Even so there is always Joy to be found in Gratitude.
Focus on that!

Peace & Love

Every single person we meet
Has something special to share with us,
To teach us,
And we them.

Peace & Love

Wake up and affirm:
'I am the best I can be.
Today I will do the best I can with
Peace, Love, and Compassion in my heart.'

Peace & Love

Every day gives us so much to be grateful for.

Peace & Love

Sometimes all you need is a little shift in perspective.

Peace & Love

Find something that gives meaning to your life,
Big or small.
That's the way forward.

Peace & Love

A challenge:
How many kind actions can you achieve in one day?
How many kind thoughts can you manifest in one day?

Peace & Love

How you define yourself has a huge impact
On how you perceive the world
And how life unfolds before you.

Peace & Love

Love without limits.
Live without fears.
Each thought makes every moment what it is,
Thus, life unfolds.

Peace & Love

Now is the time to do what you think
You should, could, ought to!

Peace & Love

Heartfelt gratitude goes to the brave of heart,
And strong of mind,
To the many giving their Lives for our Freedom and Peace.

Peace & Love

Sometimes being forced to be still can produce great works.

Peace & Love

There is only one thing you need in life:
Love.

Peace & Love

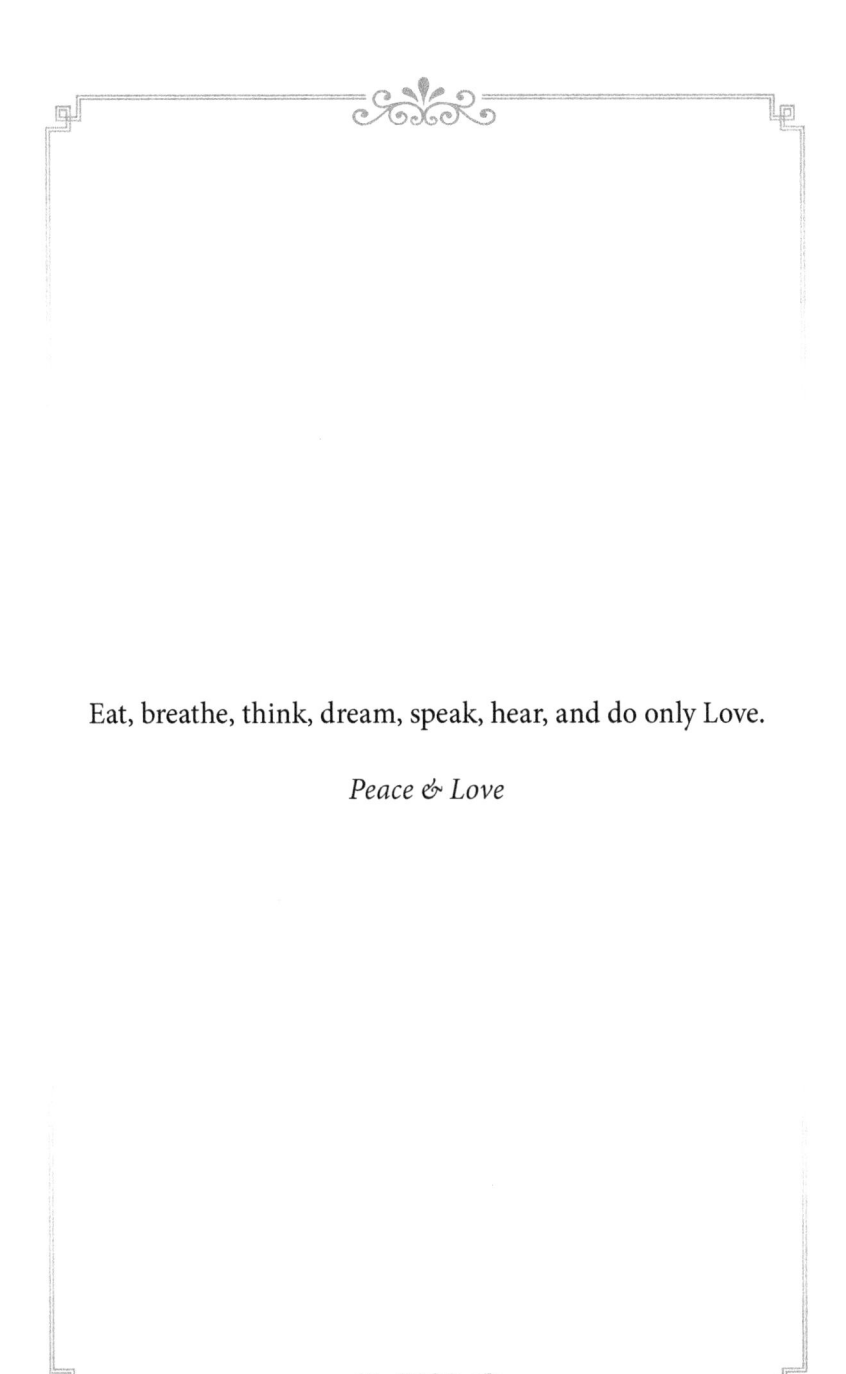

Eat, breathe, think, dream, speak, hear, and do only Love.

Peace & Love

It really is all about The Love.

Peace & Love

Believe in you! You are Beautiful.
You are Love personified.

Peace & Love

A new day has begun!
A great excuse to make your life just the way you want it.
One action of love at a time.

Peace & Love

You hold the universe within you.
Create, Be, Do, Say, Live, Laugh,
And above all Love everything.

Peace & Love

Opening your heart to the possibilities
Allows life to move forward.
Life is good.
People are helpful.
Dreams do come true.

Peace & Love

Open your heart to Gratitude and allow Grace in.
When you do,
Life provides you Love and Space.

Peace & Love

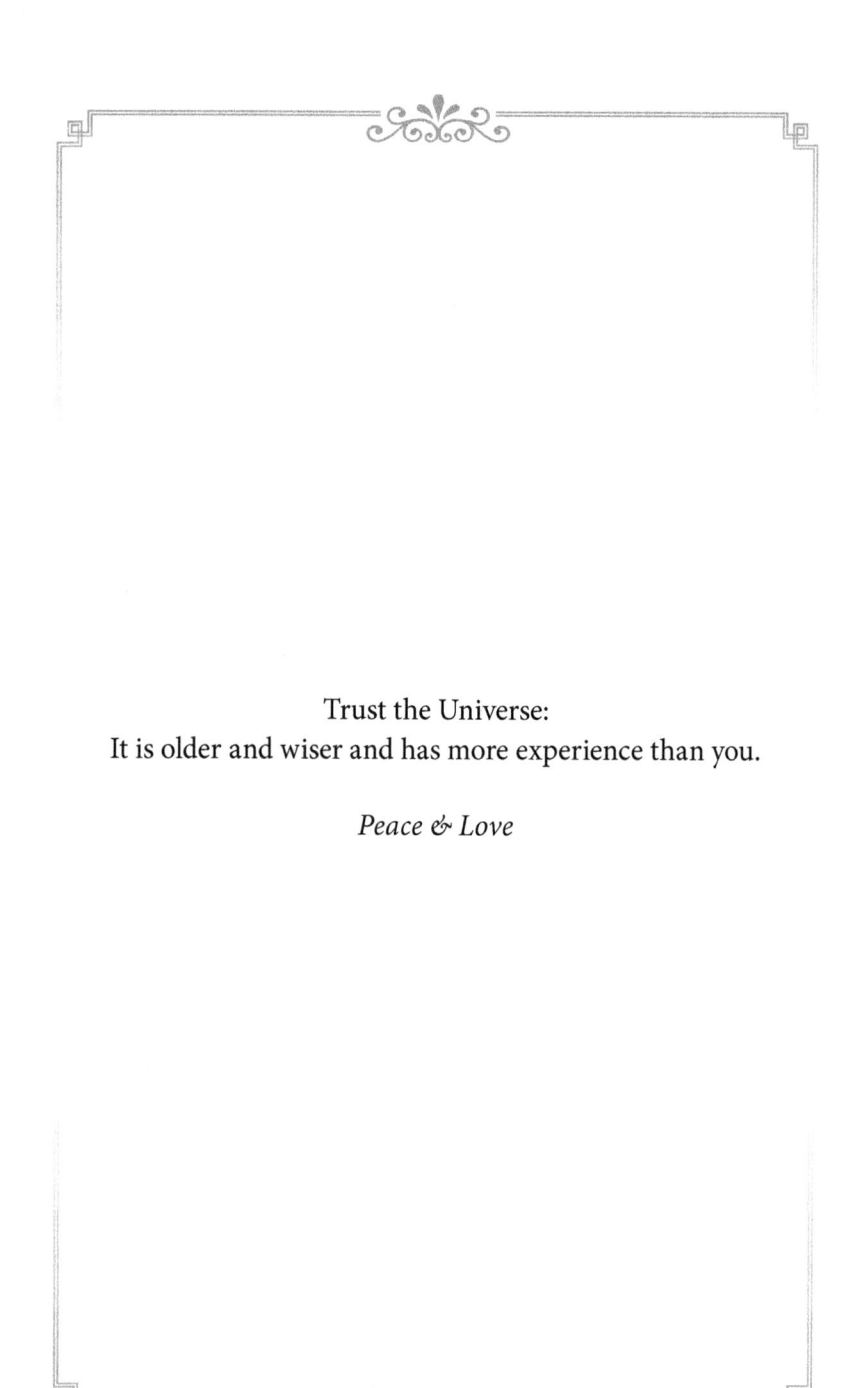

Trust the Universe:
It is older and wiser and has more experience than you.

Peace & Love

Hold true to who you are and what you want.
It will come to pass.

Peace & Love

You hold the world within you.
You are part of everything, and everything is part of You.

Peace & Love

By becoming a Master of your Thoughts,
You become the Master of your Life.
Thinking beautiful Thoughts manifests a beautiful Life.

Peace & Love

You are me, and I am you,
We are everything and everyone.
The universe is One.

Peace & Love

There is mental process: the intelligence of the mind.
There is emotional process: the intelligence of the heart.
There is understanding of who you really are.
These are the parts of self to nurture and cultivate.
Release desire and grasping, they only bring suffering.

Peace & Love

Teaching only Love means using only
Actions, speech, thoughts, and words
Of Love.

Peace & Love

Relinquish fear.
It inhibits greatness.
You are great and wonderful and born to shine.

Peace & Love

You are what you will yourself to be.
Your Life is the manifestation of your
Thoughts and Imagination.

Peace & Love

Positivity creates Positivity.
Love creates Love.
Peace creates Peace.
We are One.

Peace & Love

Have Faith in yourself.
Have Faith in your dreams.
The Universe is bountiful, and Life is magical.

Peace & Love

Every day presents itself as an opportunity
To make someone Smile,
And feel Good about who they are.

Peace & Love

When something causes a negative response,
Take a moment to understand, realise and release it.
Give Love for everything else, and Peace follows.

Peace & Love

Nature has life sussed.
If you want to understand your inner power and potential,
Sit quietly in nature, take note, and
Be Present.

Peace & Love

Sometimes you simply need to take time to be.
Find your equilibrium,
Then take on the world!

Peace & Love

Take a stance of Collaboration, Curiosity, and Tolerance.
Its kinder and healthier,
Than competition or judgement.

Peace & Love

Know what your dreams are,
In detail,
Then set out to achieve them.

Peace & Love

There is much Joy in Friendship!
Be sure to thank your Friends,
For making your heart overflow with Love.

Peace & Love

There is nothing more sacred
Nor more powerful,
Than your Love for your child.
Be Kind to your parents:
They were always doing the best they could,
With what they had,
And who they were at the time.

Peace & Love

Love, love, love with all your might!
It's the Only thing that matters in life.

Peace & Love

You create your Life with every Thought and every Deed.
You are a Creator,
Use your Power wisely and compassionately.

Peace & Love

You are what you think you are.
Your life is what you have made it.
Seize this moment to be who and what you really want to be.
Live the life you really want to live.

Peace & Love

The person who deserves
The most love, compassion, and gratitude
In your life is
YOU.

Peace & Love

You can will yourself to be happy,
And the more you do,
The more you create the habit of happiness,
Which will become your default setting.

Peace & Love

I want you to really understand
Your power,
Your potential,
Your worth.
Take a moment,
Realise how miraculous it is that you exist.
Imagine,
What had to occur,
Throughout time and space,
For this very moment to exist?
Now that is extraordinary,
And so are You.

Peace & Love

You are meant to SHINE in this life.
You are meant to be Radiant, Glorious, Beautiful.
Go out into Life,
Seize the moment,
Be who you truly are.
This Life is but Once.

Peace & Love

Kindness is underrated.
Be Kind.

Peace & Love

About the Author

Kirstie Shapiro lives with her daughter in Cambridge, UK. She holds a BSc (Hons) degree and writes on subjects of healthy living, well-being, and living life to its fullest. She lives by her words and hopes that she leads by example with Love, Grace, and Gratitude with every step she takes in life.

> *'Mother, daughter, sister, friend, human being and totally loving it.'*
> Kirstie Shapiro